Molly Pitcher:
An American Hero

by Courtney Burke
Illustrated by Paule Trudel

PEARSON

Glenview, Illinois • Boston, Massachusetts • Chandler, Arizona
Upper Saddle River, New Jersey

Molly Pitcher

Molly Pitcher is a hero of the Revolutionary War. This war was for America's freedom.

Molly's real name was Mary Hays. She was born in the mid-1700s. She grew up on a farm.

Molly wanted to be a soldier.

Molly worked for a general, an important leader.
She lived with his family. She took care of the house.

Molly heard the general's war stories. She wanted to
be a soldier. But long ago, women could not be soldiers.

Revolutionary War soldiers

When Molly was older, she married John Hays. He joined the army. He went to fight in the Revolutionary War. For months, Molly did not see her husband.

A gunner in the Revolutionary War

One day, Molly got a letter. John asked her to move to her parents' home. He was nearby with the army. So Molly moved to New Jersey.

On June 28, 1778, there was a big battle. John was a gunner. He fired a cannon.

Molly carries water to the soldiers.

Molly wanted to help. She went to the battle. It was dangerous.

Hurt soldiers lay on the ground. They needed water. So Molly carried pitchers of water to them. That is how she got the name "Molly Pitcher."

Then a British soldier shot her husband.

Molly fires the cannon.

Molly saw that John was hurt. But he was still alive. The battle was still going on. So Molly fired the cannon. She was almost shot. But she did not stop firing.

That night, the British soldiers left. The Americans had won!

Every year, people act out the battle.

Molly was a hero! George Washington gave her an award.

Today, people remember how brave Molly was. They act out the battle. Men dress in soldiers' clothes. They fire cannons. One woman plays the part of Molly Pitcher.